W9-CAD-950

HOW TO LOOK AFTER YOUR PET

BIRDS

Mark Evans

B.Vet.Med.

Angus&Robertson
An imprint of HarperCollinsPublishers

A DORLING KINDERSLEY BOOK

Project Editor Liza Bruml
Art Editor Sarah Ponder
Editor Miriam Farbey
Photographer Paul Bricknell
Additional photography Frank Greenaway
and Cyril Laubscher
Illustrator Peter Visscher

AN ANGUS & ROBERTSON BOOK
An imprint of HarperCollinsPublishers

First published in Australia in 1993 by
CollinsAngus&Robertson Publishers Pty Limited
A division of HarperCollinsPublishers (Australia) Pty Limited
25 Ryde Road, Pymble NSW 2073, Australia

HarperCollinsPublishers (New Zealand) Limited
31 View Road, Glenfield, Auckland 10, New Zealand

National Library of Australia
Cataloguing-in-Publication data:

Evans, Mark, 1962 Dec. 9 –
  Birds
  Includes index.
  ISBN 0 207 17653 1.
  1. Birds – Juvenile literature. 2. Birds, Ornamental –
  Juvenile literature.
  I. Title. (Series:How to look after your pet).
636.6

First published in Great Britain in 1993 by
Dorling Kindersley Limited, 9 Henrietta Street,
London WC2E 8PS

Colour reproduction by Colourscan, Singapore
Printed and bound by Arnoldo Mondadori, Verona, Italy

5 4 3 2 1
97 96 95 94 93

Models: Jacob Brubert, Adam Conduct, Arron Daubney,
Luke Harris, Naoka Hoshika, Sarah-Louise Hurtley, Fiona
Lala, Nicola Mason, Carlie and Lee Nicolls, Danny O'Sullivan,
Kim and Lee Robertson

Dorling Kindersley would like to thank Ernie Sigston for
providing budgies and equipment, Concepta Keenan for lending
her budgie, The Junior Bird League, Pedigree Pet Foods for
supplying bird seed, Tracy White for design help, Salvo
Tomasselli for the world map and Lynn Bresler for the index.

Picture credits: OSF/RJB Goodale Ace Films Australia p12 tr

Note to parents
This book teaches your child how to
a caring and responsible pet owner. But
remember, your child must have your
help and guidance in every aspect of day-
to-day pet care. Don't let your child keep
birds unless you are sure that your family
has the time and resources to look after
them properly – for the whole of
their lives.

KN

AFZ 3219

Contents

Introduction

The first step to becoming a good bird owner is to choose the right number and kind of pets. Budgies are the easiest to look after. A budgie likes to have company, so you should get at least two. But remember, whatever kinds and however many pets you choose, you'll need to look after them every day. Not just to start with, but for the whole of their lives.

Shopping basket full of things you will need

Understanding your pets

You have to get to know your birds. If you handle them gently and talk to them as much as you can, they will quickly learn to trust you. Watch them very carefully and you will soon begin to understand the many fascinating things that they do.

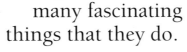

Budgies sleep with their heads tucked into their wings

Your birds enjoy a weekly shower

Caring for your pets

You will only be your pets' best friend if you care for them properly. They need water, the right food and lots of flying exercise every day. You will have to clean the cage regularly and spray your birds once a week.

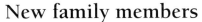

Taking your hobby further

Once you have learnt how to look after budgies, you may want to start to keep other kinds of pet birds. If you have a space outside, you could set up an aviary.

Fawn penguin zebra finches make good pets

People to help

The best bird-keeper always tries to find out more about her pets. The vet and nurse at your local vet centre will check that your birds are healthy. Ask them anything you like about how to keep your birds fit and happy.

You should visit your vet centre often

New family members

Your birds will be a special part of your whole family. Everyone will want to join in training and looking after them. Your birds may become friends with other small pets. You can also introduce them to friends that like animals.

Your birds will be part of your family

Ask a grown-up

When you see this sign in the book, you should ask an adult to help you.

Things to remember

When you live with pet birds, there are some important rules you should follow:

🐦 Never allow your pet birds to fly free outside.

🐦 Wash your hands after handling your birds or cleaning their cage.

🐦 Don't kiss your birds.

🐦 Always handle your birds very gently.

🐦 Teasing your birds is cruel.

🐦 Don't give your birds food from your plate.

🐦 Never, ever hit your birds

What is a bird?

Birds belong to a large group of animals that have a backbone, called vertebrates. All birds are warm-blooded and their young hatch from eggs. Their light bodies are covered with feathers. They have wings instead of arms, which they usually use for flying. They take off, steer and land with more control than any aeroplane. Birds can be all sorts of shapes and sizes. The most popular pet bird, the budgerigar, or budgie, belongs to a group of birds called parrots. All parrots have short, hooked beaks for cracking open seeds.

Wing is powered by strong chest muscles

Wing flaps to keep the bird up and moving

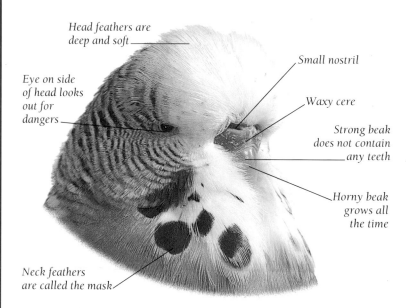

Head feathers are deep and soft

Small nostril

Eye on side of head looks out for dangers

Waxy cere

Strong beak does not contain any teeth

Horny beak grows all the time

Neck feathers are called the mask

Built to fly

A budgie is perfectly made for flying. Its streamlined body has hollow bones and its skull contains air spaces to make it light. A budgie has a special way of breathing that allows it to get a lot of oxygen to its main flight muscles. These large muscles power the wings to lift the bird into the air. The feathers that make up a bird's plumage are called tail, body, wing and down feathers.

Super senses

A bird has keen eyesight to make sure that it doesn't bump into things when flying fast. It has very good hearing, although you can't see its ear flaps. The cere, the waxy swelling at the top of its beak, has two small holes that are its nostrils. But budgies have a poor sense of smell and taste.

Long, pointed tail feathers are used for steering and to keep the bird stable

Short secondary flight
feathers give the wing a
smooth, curved surface

Long primary
feathers steer
and power flight

Fluffy down feathers
help to keep the
bird warm

Stubby alula
helps to keep
the wing stable

Black stripes are
called bars

Pointed head
is a stream-
lined shape

Black markings are
called neck spots

Eye has white
iris ring

Smooth body
feathers are
waterproof

Legs are held
close to the body

Legs are
covered in
scaly skin

Small tail
feathers fan
out to act as
a brake

Claws dig
into perch

Wings are held
neatly against
the body

Long tail is
used for
balance

The huge ostrich
cannot fly

A penguin swims with
paddle-shaped wings

A duck uses its webbed
back feet like flippers

Perfect wings let the
swift stay in the air
for months at a time

The gorgeous colours in
the male peacock's tail
attract a mate

Perching

A budgie lands on a
branch to rest, or perch.
Each leg has four claws. Two claws
face forwards and two face backwards
to give the bird a strong grip. A bird
can even perch upside down!

11

Life in the wild

Wild budgerigars live in the dry grasslands of Australia. They are nomadic, which means that they never settle in one place. Nearly all wild budgies are yellow and green coloured so they are hidden when they feed in grass. They live in large groups, called flocks. Although the budgie is the most popular pet bird, it is not the only one. Over thousands of years many kinds of wild birds, from all over the world, have been tamed.

Finding food and drink
Budgies eat wild grass seeds and drink from desert pools in the cool early morning and evening. The flocks fly from place to place in search of food and water.

Life in the flock
A flock of budgies may have only 20 birds, but if food or water is scarce, thousands of birds will join together. A large group is better at protecting itself from enemies and finding food and water. The flock sleeps, or roosts, in the safety of the high branches.

Small, wild budgie is yellow and green

Pets from around the world

The wild relatives of pet birds come from all the continents of the world. African canaries are popular because they sing beautifully. The blue-fronted Amazon parrot is striking, but can be noisy and difficult to look after. Many birds kept as pets are now endangered species. Never buy a bird that has been caught in the wild.

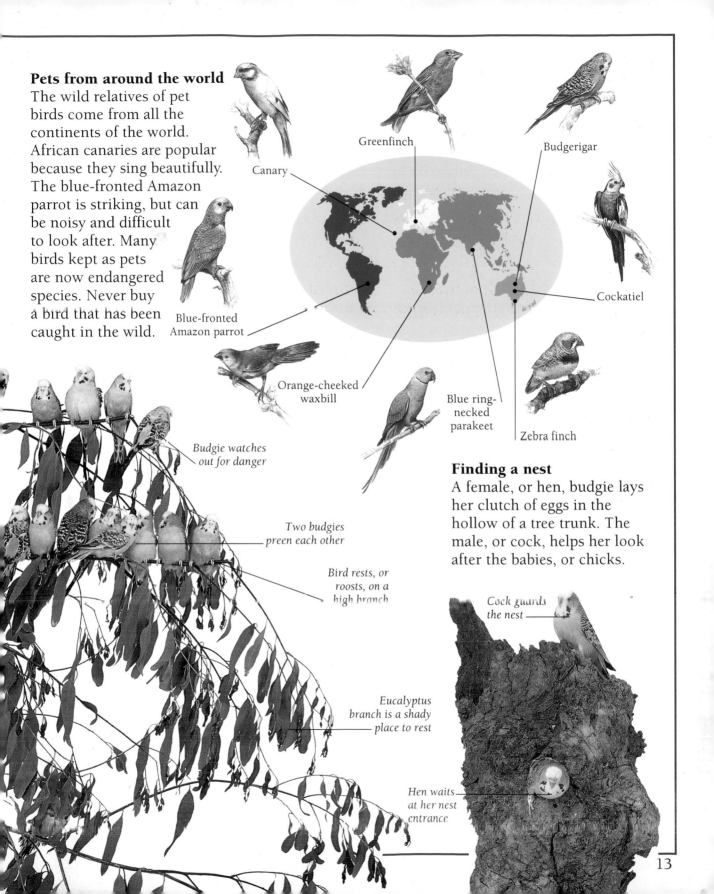

Canary

Greenfinch

Budgerigar

Cockatiel

Blue-fronted Amazon parrot

Orange-cheeked waxbill

Blue ring-necked parakeet

Zebra finch

Budgie watches out for danger

Two budgies preen each other

Bird rests, or roosts, on a high branch

Eucalyptus branch is a shady place to rest

Finding a nest

A female, or hen, budgie lays her clutch of eggs in the hollow of a tree trunk. The male, or cock, helps her look after the babies, or chicks.

Cock guards the nest

Hen waits at her nest entrance

13

Types of budgie

The first people to keep budgies noticed that some chicks had unusual markings and feather colours. By choosing which of these to breed, the bird-keepers created different types of budgie. Today, there are hundreds of types. They can be divided into groups according to their colour and markings.

Yellow forehead

Yellow and green wings with black markings

Light green

The wild budgie
Most wild budgies are green with black wing markings and yellow faces. All green budgies have yellow faces.

Other normals
Budgies with black wing markings are called normals. Their bodies can be different colours, such as grey or blue. They can have either white or yellow faces.

Cinnamon violet

Brown lines on wings

Cinnamon sky-blue

Throat spots are brown

Light grey chest

White head

Normal sky-blue

Normal grey

Deep blue chest

Pink feet

Cinnamon grey green

Cinnamon light green

Bright yellow face

Violet body

Normal cobalt

Cinnamon grey

Normal yellow-faced violet

Tail is cinnamon

Cinnamons
Some budgies have brown markings on their wings and throat spots. They are called cinnamons. Their bodies can be any colour but they are not as bright as normals.

Greywings

Greywing budgies are rare. They have grey instead of black wing markings. Their bodies are different colours, but are always very pale.

Fine grey lines on wing

Pale sky-blue body

Grey feet

Greywinged sky-blue

Long light blue tail

White band

Faint black markings

Cere has pink tinge

Black-tipped wing feathers

Sky-blue dominant pied

White patch

Opaline violet

Cinnamon grey dominant pied

Violet recessive pied

Light green spangle

Red eye

Pink cere

White body

Pink feet

Albino

White cheek patch

Body patterns

The dominant pied budgie has patches or a band of a different colour. The cere and feet of a recessive pied are tinted with pink and it has no iris ring. A budgie with faint black markings on its neck, back and the rear of its head is called an opaline. The spangle has dark-edged pale wing feathers.

Lutino

White tail

A single colour

All the feathers of the albino are white. Its eyes, cere and feet are pink. The lutino is completely yellow apart from its tail, cheeks and wing tips.

Yellow face

Brown spots

White-edged throat spots

Dark-edged wing feather

Amazing mixtures

Some birds look interesting as they have a mixture of many features. They are impossible to put together in one class.

Yellow-laced albino

Yellow-faced opaline cinnamon sky blue

Opaline spangle cobalt

Your budgies' home

Your budgies need a large cage to live in so they have plenty of room to stretch their wings. Put the cage in a safe place in your living room, where your budgies will often have company. You will also need to buy feeding equipment, lining material for the cage trays and a cage cover. Stock up with food and find branches to use as perches.

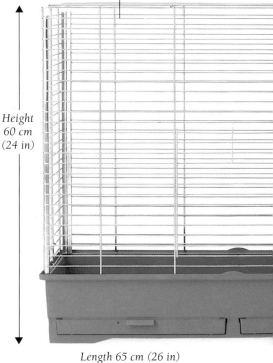

Bars are 10 mm (³/8 in) apart to stop your birds poking their heads through

Height 60 cm (24 in)

Length 65 cm (26 in)

The cage
Look at the measurements in the picture. Your pets' cage should be at least this big, and wider than it is tall so that your birds can fly between the perches. The cage bars must be horizontal so your birds can exercise by climbing them.

Lining paper

Bird sand-sheet

Wood shavings

Storage bin

Scoop

Bird sand

Lining the cage
Buy paper and wood shavings to line the trays. To give your birds something different to stand on sometimes, get bird sand-sheets or sand.

Fruit tree perch
Find branches for perches that are at least 10 mm (³/8 in) wide.

Cage cover
Make or buy a cover to put over the cage so your birds can rest.

Check the measurements of a cage before buying it

Tray slides open so cage lining can be easily replaced

Water drinker

Feeding perch

Jam-jar seed hopper

Fresh food tray

Grit hopper

Feeding equipment
You will need containers for water, seed, grit and fresh food. Buy hoppers with perches for your birds to stand on while they eat.

Clips
Buy some clips to attach food and the cuttlefish to the cage bars.

Food and minerals
Buy an all-in-one budgerigar seed mixture, soluble grit, cuttlefish and a small iodine block. Store the seed and grit in air-tight containers. You will also need to feed fresh foods (see p25).

Cuttlefish

Iodine block

Spinach leaf

Air-tight container

Seed mixture

Grit

Where to put your budgies' cage

Put the cage high up where budgies feel safe

Make sure your pets are in a smoke-free place

Don't use a spray near the cage

Keep the cage out of bright sunlight

Draughts will upset your birds

Make sure other pets can't reach the cage

Things to get ready

You will need some special equipment to help you look after your new pets. You can find some things around your house, and have fun making others. Make sure you have got all the things ready before you fetch your budgies. Once you have become an experienced bird-keeper you may want to get an aviary to put in the garden.

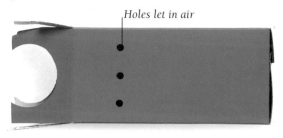

Holes let in air

Carrying box
You will need a small, cardboard carrying box in which to take each of your budgies home.

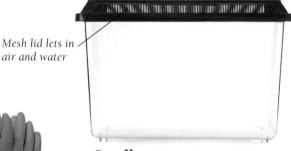

Mesh lid lets in air and water

Cleaning equipment
You will need special things to clean your budgies' cage. Never take things that are used to clean your house. Ask your vet what kind of disinfectant spray to buy.

Bucket

Sponge

Rubber gloves

Small cage
Buy a plastic tank with a mesh lid to put your pets in when you want to clean their cage thoroughly. You can also use the tank when you want to spray your budgies with water (see p43).

Detergent

Scrubbing brush

Bottle brush

Scraper

Disinfectant spray

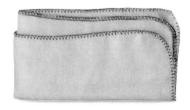

Duster
Get a large, clean duster. You will need to throw this over a bird if it escapes.

Bird toys

Budgies love to play. Find and make toys for them. They will enjoy climbing on an activity centre while they are flying free in a room (see p36). You can put other small toys in their cage.

Activity centre

Wooden ball

Fir cone

Wooden abacus

The aviary

You can build or buy an outdoor aviary to create a more natural home for your birds. It should have a shed for the birds to shelter in and a large flight area. You can keep many birds together in an aviary (see p34).

Plant sprayer

Splash cover hood

Hooks to fix bath over door opening

Bird bath

Weighing scales

You will need to weigh your budgies regularly to check that they are healthy. Find old, small kitchen scales and paper to line the tray.

Paper tray lining

Bathing equipment

Budgies like to bathe. Buy a bath with a splash cover hood that fits on a door of the cage. Also get a plant sprayer to shower your birds with in the tank.

Free-flying equipment

Get fine netting to put over all the windows and any fireplaces, and rubber suckers to stick perches onto the walls.

Rubber suckers

Fine netting

Choosing your birds

A budgie likes company, so you should get at least two to keep in the same cage. You can buy baby budgies, or chicks, from a clutch when they are at least six weeks old. Adult budgies also make good pets, but you must get two that are already good friends. Whichever budgies you choose, check that they are healthy.

Where to buy your birds:

🐦 An animal shelter may have birds of all kinds and ages that need new homes.

🐦 A breeder will sell you chicks that are six weeks old.

🐦 A friend's birds may have chicks.

1 **When you go to choose** your birds, watch the chicks with the owner. Try not to disturb them. Check that the birds are well looked after. The cage should be clean and hoppers full.

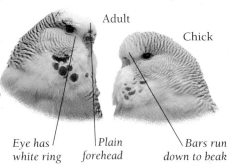

Adult

Chick

Eye has white ring *Plain forehead* *Bars run down to beak*

Getting two budgies

A budgie will be lonely living on its own. You can choose two males or two females. Males are often easier to tame. Don't worry if you find that you have chosen a male and a female. They are unlikely to have babies in your cage.

Young or old?

It is easy to tell the age of a budgie. It has fine black lines, or bars, down to its beak until it is three months old. An adult budgie has no bars on its forehead and a white ring in its eye.

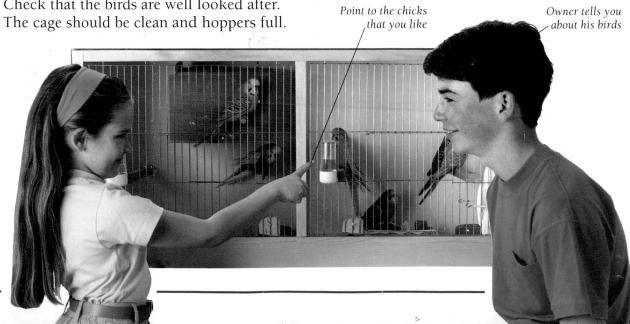

Point to the chicks that you like

Owner tells you about his birds

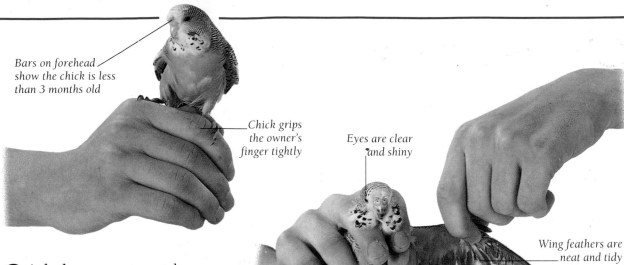

Bars on forehead show the chick is less than 3 months old

Chick grips the owner's finger tightly

Eyes are clear and shiny

Wing feathers are neat and tidy

2 **Ask the owner** to catch a bird that you like, and to tell you its sex. It should look bright and alert. Check that the bird is the right age to be taken home and that it hasn't been chosen by someone else.

Feathers under the bird's tail are clean

3 **Check that the bird** is healthy. It should have bright eyes, a smooth beak and clean feathers all over its body. Ask the owner to hold out each of the wings so you can make sure they aren't damaged.

Owner carefully lifts the bird into its box

Hold the carrying box still

Tightly closed box contains your other bird

4 **The owner will put** the birds you choose into your special carrying boxes. Shut the lids properly so the birds can't escape. They will breathe the fresh air that comes in through the holes. Take your new pets to your vet centre on your way home, so your vet can give them a check-up.

Welcome home

Your birds may be frightened when they leave their brothers and sisters. To help them settle into their new home, have everything prepared in the cage. If you already have a budgie and are introducing a new friend, watch them when they first meet. It is a good idea to cover the cage at first to make your birds feel more relaxed.

Use your scoop to lift the shavings

Lining paper is folded to fit

1 **Fill both of the cage trays** with wood shavings after lining them with paper. The wood shavings and paper will help soak up any spilt water and moist droppings.

Put the perches far apart so that the birds have space to fly

Branch is high, where birds like to perch

2 **Wedge perching** branches between the front and back of the cage. Put one perch high up at each end of the cage and a third perch lower down.

3 **Pour grit into the grit hopper** after filling the seed hopper and water drinker. Also prepare a selection of fresh food (see p25). Put the hoppers and fresh food in the cage. Do not put them under the perches, or bird droppings will fall into them.

Fresh food treats make the birds feel at home

Pour grit until the hopper is full

Hopper is filled with seed mixture

Water seeps into tray until it is full

Iodine block is
fixed high up
the cage

Millet spray for
birds to peck

Bird has settled
on a high perch

Bird bath is
full of water

Wire cage sits
securely on
the base

Cuttlefish is
clipped to
the bars

Water drinker
is near a perch

Seed hopper
is out of the
way of the
perch above

Dish of fresh
food is on the
cage floor

Lined tray
slides in and
out of the
cage base

4 **Release your birds into their cage** when you have finished
preparing it. Open each carrying box inside the cage and let your
bird climb out. Then spread the cover over the cage. Your birds will
feel calmer in dim light and be keener to explore their new home.

Male or female?

Ask your vet to check
the sex of your budgies.
A young male or cock
is larger than a young
female or hen. An
adult male has a blue
cere – a soft, waxy
swelling at the
top of the beak.

Hen

Cock

Young cock is bigger
than young hen

Adult hen has
a brown cere

Adult cock
has a blue cere

5 **You should arrange** to
visit your vet centre
on the way home from
collecting your new pets.
The vet will examine each
bird to make
sure that it
is healthy.

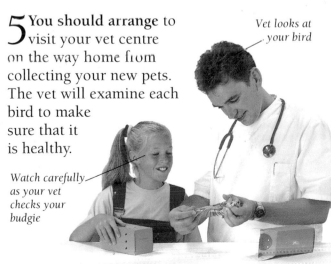

Vet looks at
your bird

Watch carefully
as your vet
checks your
budgie

Feeding your budgies

Like many birds, budgies are omnivores. This means they eat plants as well as meat. In the wild, budgies feed mainly on different kinds of grass seed. They pick up scattered seeds from the ground or peck at flower heads. As well as feeding seed from the hopper, you can scatter some seed on the cage floor.

Red millet

Seed mixture

White millet

Grit

Canary seed

Pour fresh seed into the jam-jar

How much to feed
You should make sure that your birds always have seed to eat. Fill the hopper with seed from the container.

Basic diet
You should feed your pets grit and a specially prepared mixture of seeds that contains essential vitamins and minerals.

When to feed
Check how full the seed hopper is every evening. When the hopper jar is nearly empty, throw away the remaining seed and refill it with enough fresh seed to last your birds about one week.

Fresh water
Wild budgerigars get some water from the food they eat, and they also drink from pools. You must make sure that your pets always have fresh water to drink in their drinker.

Your budgie will eat most in the morning and evening

The bird stands on the perch to feed from the hopper

Drinker is easily reached from the perch

Budgie can drink whenever it is thirsty

*Strong beak is used
to crack seeds
before they are
swallowed*

*Bird stands on
hopper perch*

*Hopper is filled
with grit*

*Cuttlefish bone contains
the mineral calcium,
which your birds need
to keep healthy*

*Block contains
the essential
mineral iodine*

Grit

Make sure that the grit hopper is always full. Budgies don't have teeth – they break open the hard seed coats with their beaks. Your budgies swallow grit to help them grind up the tough seeds in their stomachs.

Cuttlefish

Keep a piece of cuttlefish bone clipped to the cage bars. Your budgies will peck the cuttlefish to get any extra calcium that they need. Fix the iodine block to the cage bars for your birds to nibble.

Fresh foods

Fresh fruit and vegetables are full of goodness. Offer different kinds to your birds to find out which they like best. Clip a spray of dried millet to the cage bars. Your budgie will enjoy pecking seeds from the spray.

Millet spray

Apple   Pear   Raspberries

Alfalfa   Celery   Peas

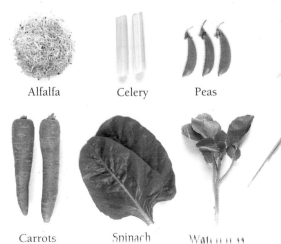

*Tame budgie perches on
the tray edge to feed*

Carrots   Spinach   Watercress

How much to feed

👥 Once a day, prepare a handful of fruit and vegetables cut into large chunks. Place the chopped up food on a tray on the cage floor.

Handling your birds

All budgies are frightened of people to start with. The more time you spend with your pets, the quicker they will learn to trust you. Start to tame them straight away by talking to them. You can train them to perch on your finger. Repeat each of the following steps until your bird is used to it. Then go onto the next.

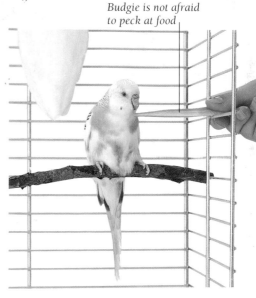

Budgie is not afraid to peck at food

1 **Wedge a piece** of your budgie's favourite fresh food between the cage bars. Your budgie will not fly away because it will want to nibble the food. It will soon become used to your hand being close to it.

Stroke the feathers gently

Bird pecks at the fresh food

2 **Put your hand** inside the cage while your budgie is eating the food stuck between the bars. Stroke the bird's neck with your finger. It should not be worried by you because it is busy eating. Do not make any sudden hand movements that could startle your bird.

Hold the perch very still

3 **Slowly move a perch** with food clipped on it towards your budgie. Your bird will be tempted onto the perch by the food. It may be shy at first and just put one foot on the perch. Be patient and keep trying.

Holding your birds

Pick up and hold your budgie in cupped hands if you want to look at it closely. It will grip your fingers with its claws. Hold your bird quite firmly to make it feel safe.

Hold firmly but don't squeeze your bird

When to handle your new pets

Days 1-2: Watch your pets carefully but do not disturb them. Keep half of their cage covered.

Day 3: Start to feed your pets by hand through the cage bars. Pick your birds up in cupped hands if you need to.

Days 4-14: Handle your pets several times a day for a short period of time, following the handling steps.

After two weeks: Play with your pets and talk to them at least twice a day.

4 **Now your bird** should be ready to sit on your finger instead of the hand-held perch. Move your first finger slowly towards your bird. Your pet should be happy to climb onto your finger.

Claws grip your finger – but it doesn't hurt!

Hold your finger still so your pet finds this new perch stable

Budgie waits to be taken out of its cage

Point your finger slightly upwards – your pet will move to the highest point of its perch

5 **When your budgie** is happy to sit on your finger you can take it out of the cage. Make sure the room is safe (see p32). If you feel your bird raise its wings, stop moving and let it settle. Now you can begin training your pets to fly to and from your hand.

Understanding your pets

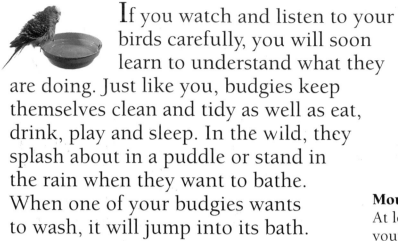

If you watch and listen to your birds carefully, you will soon learn to understand what they are doing. Just like you, budgies keep themselves clean and tidy as well as eat, drink, play and sleep. In the wild, they splash about in a puddle or stand in the rain when they want to bathe. When one of your budgies wants to wash, it will jump into its bath.

Body feather looks ruffled

Moulting
At least once a year, your budgies will lose their feathers, or moult. Feathers that are broken or damaged are replaced. Your pets will look very scruffy when they are moulting, but they are not ill.

Tail feathers are ragged

New feathers stick up out of plumage

Wet feathers stick out in all directions

Smooth head is already dry

Nimble bird can bend to preen under its wing

Preened feathers are sleek

Beak nibbles and strokes feather back into shape

All puffed up
After having a shower or getting wet in the bath, your budgie moves its body from side to side to shake off the water. It fluffs up its feathers to keep warm. The fluffy feathers make a very warm coat.

Preening
You will often see your budgie preening, or cleaning itself with its beak. While preening, your bird spreads a thin layer of oil from a gland under its tail to waterproof its feathers.

Gnawing natural perches

Your budgie will peck the bark on its perch looking for insects. Gnawing helps to keep its beak from getting too long.

Pointed beak gnaws the bark

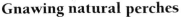 Making noises

Budgies make all kinds of sounds. Chicks call to their parents with a loud, high-pitched trill. Happy budgies chirp, but they will stop if disturbed. Budgies are good mimics. They can learn to say words or even copy a ringing telephone!

Showing friendship

Your two birds will be best friends. They will chirp to each other and play together. You will often see them helping each other to groom tricky places.

Budgie bends its head to the side

Budgie nibbles at its friend's neck feathers

Climbing

Like all members of the parrot family, budgies are good climbers. By using its beak as a hook, your budgie can move its feet without falling. Your birds will spend a lot of time climbing the bars of their cage.

Beak grips perch

Claws clasp branch

Budgie tucks its head under a wing

Sleeping

When your budgies are asleep, or roosting, they shut their eyes and fluff up their feathers to keep warm. A sleeping budgie regularly opens its eyes to check it is not in danger.

Cleaning the cage

Your budgies like their home to be very clean. If the cage becomes dirty, it will start to smell and your pets will become ill. You should tidy the cage and replace dirty litter, check the seed hopper is not blocked, and wash the drinker every day. Throw away uneaten fresh food. Once a week, scrub out the cage thoroughly. Replace any perches that are worn or broken.

Leave the lining paper unless it is torn or very dirty

Use the scraper to remove the dirty litter

Close your eyes when you blow

Hold the hopper up to your face

1 **Every day**, scrape out any dirty litter from the cage trays. Top up the trays with fresh wood shavings. If you use sand-sheets, replace them daily.

2 **Blow the tough seed shells**, called husks, from the seed hopper. Your birds crack the husks off seeds before they eat the seed inside. The husks settle on uneaten seed in the hopper tray.

Push the bottle brush to the end of the tube

Flying husks can make a mess

3 **Clean the inside of the drinker** after throwing away any old water. Then refill the drinker with fresh water.

Close the lid tightly

Bird can firmly grip the sand-sheet

1 **Once a week**, put your budgies into their small tank. Catch them in cupped hands or by using your duster (see p33). Then take out the hoppers, food and perches. Unclip anything from the bars. Throw away all the wood shavings and lining paper.

2 **Scrub the cage trays** with hot, soapy water. Dry them with a paper towel, then spray the insides with the special disinfectant. Leave the trays to dry before refilling them with litter.

Wipe the inside of the jar carefully

Special disinfectant is safe for your birds

Washing-up liquid

Rubber gloves keep your hands clean

3 **Take out the seed hopper** and throw away any uneaten seed. Wipe the inside of the jar and the hopper tray with a damp sponge before refilling it. Don't forget to clean the fresh food tray.

Scrub all round each of the bars

4 **Clean the cage bars** with soapy water. Then spray them with a little of the disinfectant, and leave them to dry. Put the perches, bath, hoppers and some fresh food back into the cage. Remember to clip on the cuttlefish and Iodine block.

Reach into every corner of the cage

Exercising your budgies

Your birds need regular exercise to keep them healthy. Let them out in a room as soon as they are finger-tame (see p26). They should fly freely for at least 20 minutes a day. Make the room safe for your pets by covering all the windows and chimneys with netting. Never let your birds fly outside. If one of your birds won't fly back to its cage, catch it using a duster.

Swing tests bird's sense of balance

Activity centre

Ask an adult to help you make an activity centre for your birds. Climbing the ladders will strengthen the muscles in their legs and jaws.

Feathers fan out

Eye searches for another perch on which to land

Light body is easily carried by the powerful wings

Wing beats down to lift the bird up and forward

Budgie pushes off the perch with its back feet

Ready for take-off

Before you let your birds out of their cage, fix perches high up on the walls of your living room with the suckers. Put newspaper on the floor under the perches. Open the cage door and your birds will fly out. It is fun to watch them flying from perch to perch.

Rubber sucker fixes perch to wall

Cover the cage corner that has the highest perch

Throw the duster gently

Glass in windows and doors must be covered with netting

Rest after exercise

Cover the cage after your pets have exercised, and when you go to sleep at night. During the day, cover just a corner of the cage. If your pets feel tired, they can sleep in the dark area.

Catching an escaped bird

If your bird doesn't fly back to the cage turn off the lights. Find your pet and throw the duster over it. Pick it up in the duster and put the bundle in the cage.

Screen off fireplaces to stop birds flying up the chimney

Eye judges the distance to the cage

Wing is used as a brake

Body is almost upright

Foot is ready to step onto the cage

Shut dogs and cats away as they will frighten your birds

Returning home

When your bird is flying freely, leave the cage door open. Put some fresh food inside the cage. This will usually tempt your bird to fly back inside but sometimes it will land on top. Your bird knows exactly how fast to approach its cage. It uses its tail and wings as brakes. By the time it reaches the cage, it has virtually stopped. All it has to do is step onto a perch.

Some houseplants will poison your pets if they eat them

Heaters and hot drinks may burn your budgies

The aviary

Birds love to fly around in an outdoor aviary. There are interesting sounds and things for them to watch. Build an aviary with a weatherproof shelter for your birds to roost in at night. The large flying area, called the flight, should be partly covered with plastic to protect the birds from wind and rain. You can put many birds in an aviary.

Hang the feeder where it isn't in the way of flying birds

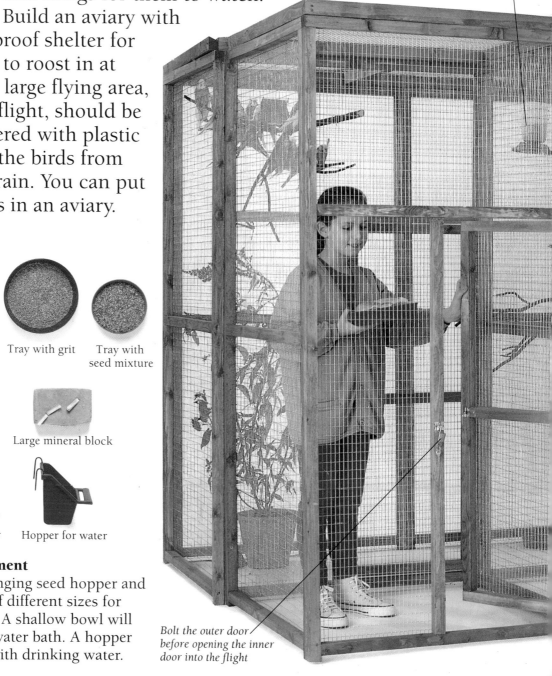

Bird bath

Tray with grit

Tray with seed mixture

Hanging hopper

Large mineral block

Hopper for water

Aviary equipment
Get a large hanging seed hopper and several trays of different sizes for seed and grit. A shallow bowl will make a good water bath. A hopper can be filled with drinking water.

Bolt the outer door before opening the inner door into the flight

The aviary

Your aviary should be at least four metres (twelve feet) long and one metre (three feet) wide. You will be able to keep up to twenty budgerigars in this size of aviary. Put fruit tree branches in the flight and shelter for perches, but make sure you leave your birds plenty of flying room.

Attach the millet spray to the mesh

Plastic protects perch from bad weather

Overhanging, sloping roof keeps shelter dry

Main perch is a branch in a flower pot

Put the bird bath under cover

Wire netting stops birds from escaping and other animals from getting in

Shelter should have perches inside for birds to roost on at night

Siting the aviary

Make sure other animals can't burrow into the aviary

Wild birds on overhanging tree will foul the flight

Put the aviary in a place sheltered from wind and rain

A noisy road will upset your birds

Position the aviary where you can see it from indoors

35

Things to do with your budgies

Look in magazines about birds, or ask at your vet centre for the address of your local pet club. If you join the junior section, you can talk to other bird owners about interesting things to do with your budgies. You can teach a budgie to talk and you can train it to fly back to your finger. Everyone will have good ideas about training your birds and making toys for them.

Bird can fly away if it gets worried

Family pets

Your budgie may make friends with other small pets. A rabbit knows that a bird is too tiny to harm it. Never leave your bird alone with another pet.

Talking budgie

You can try to train your birds to say their names. Whenever you are with one bird on its own, repeat its name over and over again.

Bird hears its name and flies to your finger

Hold your finger high

Bird perches on your hand

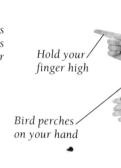

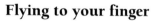

Bird cocks its head to one side to listen

Flying to your finger

Every time your birds are flying freely, practice calling them to you. Hold your hand near to where your bird is perching. Repeat its name until it flies onto your finger. In time you should be able to call your bird to you from across the room.

Step closer to the perch if your bird doesn't fly to you

Foot is used to push the ball

Wooden ball
Budgies are very curious. They will be fascinated by anything that moves. Give your birds a small wooden ball and they will play their own sort of carpet football!

Budgie stares at the moving disc

Bird slides the disc with its foot

Toy abacus
Make your birds an abacus from a rod and several wooden discs. Your budgies will enjoy shuffling the discs along the rod. Bird toys are special treats – only leave them inside the cage for a short while.

Leaving your pets

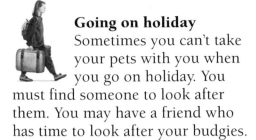

Going on holiday
Sometimes you can't take your pets with you when you go on holiday. You must find someone to look after them. You may have a friend who has time to look after your budgies.

What to pack
Get everything ready for your friend. Make sure you pack enough of all the types of food (see p24), grit, wood shavings and lining paper. Don't forget some spare perches and all the cleaning equipment.

Making a check list
Make a list of all the jobs that need doing every day. Write them down in the order that you do them. Show your friend how to do the complicated jobs. Note the name and telephone number of your vet.

Moving your birds
Take your birds to your friend in their carrying boxes. Take their cage separately. Only allow your friend to let your birds out to exercise if you are sure that they won't be able to escape, and that the windows in the room are covered with netting.

Other kinds of pet birds

You can find out which birds can be kept as pets at your vet centre. Cockatiels, canaries and finches are easy to look after. Experienced bird-keepers may train birds of prey. Some people keep racing pigeons; tame chickens and ducks often live in farmyards. Big parrots are pretty birds, but they are happiest living wild.

Feathers on head form a fluffy crest

Thick yellow and white neckband

Gloster fancy canary

Head is raised as canary warbles

Bill is closed when cock sings

Roller canary

Three toes point forward

Yellow cap

Pointed beak is perfect for cracking seeds

Speckled plumage is silky

Lizard canary

Small, round head

Bright yellow plumage

Narrow tail

Plump body

Border fancy canary

Plumage is deep red

Dark eye

Red factor canary

Tail is pale red

Short wing makes canary acrobatic in flight

Canaries

The canary, a type of finch, has been kept as a pet for hundred of years. The cocks sing beautifully. Like all finches, canaries are not as easy to handle as budgies and are difficult to hand-tame. It is best to keep a group of them in an aviary. They enjoy company and are strong fliers.

Cockatiels

Cockatiels belong to a group of small parrots called cockatoos. All cockatoos have a crest on their heads but the cocks and hens look different. Cockatiels are bigger than budgies and need more space. You can keep at least two together in a big cage or aviary. Although more timid than budgies at first, cockatiels are easy to tame.

Bright orange ear patch

Yellow head

Crest can be raised or lowered

Cockatiel hen

Cockatiel cock

Some chickens kept on farms are tamed and kept as pets

A racing pigeon can find its way home

A Harris hawk is trained to fly and hunt

Whitish-yellow plumage

Lutino cockatiel cock

Feathery crest

Hooked beak

Very long tail

Pearl markings on long wing

Pearl cockatiel cock

Orange cheek patch

Bright red bill

Grey plumage is duller than the cock's

Black and white stripes on breast

Zebra finch cock

Zebra finch hen

Lovebirds are looked after by experienced parrot-keepers

Fawn wings

White breast

Fawn penguin finch cock

Zebra finches

Zebra finches get their name from the black and white stripes on the cock's neck. Like canaries, they are timid birds that should be kept as a group in a very large cage or aviary.

Geese can be spiteful and make good guard-dogs!

Having babies

Baby birds, called chicks, hatch from eggs laid by their mother. Hen and cock birds won't breed unless you give them a special nesting box. If you have hen and cock budgies, you might think it would be fun to let them have chicks. Don't forget that breeding birds and babies need special care. The chicks will soon grow up and you will need to find them all new homes.

White eggs are the size of a thimble

1 **After mating**, a hen will usually start to lay eggs. She will lay one egg every other day until there are between four and six eggs in the clutch. The hen will sit on the eggs for 18 days to keep them warm.

Egg tooth chips at shell

Hatching chick

Heavy head is propped on an unhatched egg

Two-hour-old chick

Food can be seen in crop

Two-day-old chick

2 **Each chick breaks** through the shell using a tiny chisel-like egg tooth on top of its beak. It rests its head on the unhatched eggs. The hen feeds the chicks food from her mouth and they grow very quickly.

Two-day-old chick is completely smooth

Large bulge of food in crop

Four-day-old chick snuggles up to its older brothers and sisters

Egg has not yet hatched

Six-day-old chick is covered in very fine down

3 **All the hatched** chicks huddle next to each other to keep warm. A new chick is born every two days. The eggs in the clutch hatch out in the same order as they were laid.

Downy feathers
start to grow

23 days

Growing pinfeathers cover head

All the fluffy feathers
have now grown

Weak legs
splay out
sideways

21 days

4 At about 17 days old, the chicks start to develop their adult feathers. They are now called fledglings. When the youngest chick is 21 days old, the oldest will look like a small fluffy adult.

25 days

Chick looks almost
fully grown

27 days

Black bars run
down forehead

Mask has
clear spots

Yellow
forehead
has no bars

6 After four months, the budgie moults for the first time. It looks quite spiky as new feathers grow. The bird grooms itself to help the feathers unfold.

Mask spots
have grown
larger

5 The chicks are ready to leave the nest and go to new homes at six weeks. They can crack and eat seeds by themselves. They still can't fly properly and are a little bit wobbly when they perch.

Tail is
scruff

7 A budgie is fully adult after its first moult. A hen can lay eggs of her own when she is five months old. At six months a white ring develops in each eye, called an iris ring.

Adult feathers are
smooth and sleek

41

Health care

You need to look after your birds properly to make sure that they stay healthy. You must give them the right food (see p24), clean out their cage (see p30) and make sure they get exercise (see p32). You also need to do some health checks with your birds every day. You will learn to spot quickly if a bird is unwell.

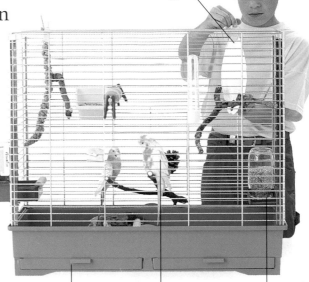

Re-clip the cuttlefish if it has slipped

1 **Every morning** when you take the cover off the cage, check that your birds are alert and active. Make sure that the hoppers and perches are still fixed tightly.

Open the trays to see if the droppings are normal

Budgie looks around curiously

Check that the hopper has not fallen

Head is held between your first and second fingers

2 **Look at your budgie's head.** The eyes should be bright and shiny and the nostrils clean. Check that the beak is smooth and not overgrown.

Carefully grip the wing between your fingers

3 **Gently pull out a wing** to check that it is not damaged. Hold the wing in the middle, not at the tip. Examine both sides of the wing. The feathers should be clean and neat.

Tail feathers are in good condition

Claw curls around your finger

Claw is the right length

Claw is too long

Budgie feels safe lying in your hand

Gently pull back the tail

4 **Check the claws** are the right length. Hold your finger under the bird's foot – the claws will grip it. Don't forget to check the two backward-pointing claws.

5 **Look under** your bird's tail by tipping it onto its back. The feathers should be clean and dry. Push back the chest feathers with your finger to see the pink skin.

Budgie perches on the edge of the tray

Paper lining keeps the tray clean

Needle shows the weight

Weighing your bird
Weigh your budgie at the same time on the same day each week. Write down the result in your pet diary. If your budgerigar has lost or gained a lot of weight, it may be ill, or it may not be getting enough exercise.

Weekly shower
When you thoroughly clean the cage and your budgies are in their small tank, give them a cold shower. Use a plant sprayer to spray your birds through the tank lid. This will keep their plumage healthy.

Spray produces a fine mist

Bird stands still to enjoy its shower

Your pet care check list
Use this list to keep a record of all the jobs you need to do.

Copy this chart. Tick off the jobs when you have finished them.

Every day:
Feed your pets

Blow seed husks from seed hopper

Wash and refill the drinker

Tidy the cage and trays

Let birds fly free

Clean underneath the cage

Examine the eyes, beak and nostrils

Look at the wings

Check the claws

◆

Once a week:
Clean the cage thoroughly

Wash and refill the seed hopper

Weigh your birds

Shower your pets

Check cuttlefish, grit and block

◆

Every year:
Take your budgies to the vet centre for a full check-up

Visiting your vet centre

The vets and nurses who work at your local vet centre know a lot about pet birds. They will tell you how to look after your birds properly to keep them happy and healthy. You can ask them as many questions as you like. If you think something is wrong with your birds, ring your vet centre immediately. The vet and nurse will try to make them better if they are ill.

Visiting the vet

Take your budgie to the vet in its carrying box. Bring the cage as well so that the vet can check it. Your vet will give your budgie health checks. If your pet is ill, the vet may give you medicine for your bird or ask you to care for it in a special way.

The cage may give the vet a clue about what is wrong with your pet

Telephoning the vet centre

Telephone the nurse at your vet centre if you want more information about pet clubs or if you think one of your birds is ill. The nurse may suggest you bring your birds to see the vet.

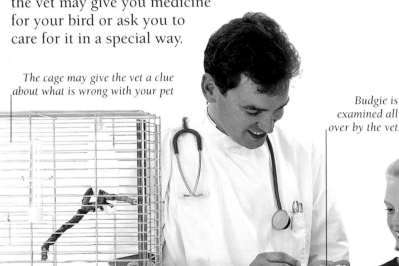

Budgie is examined all over by the vet

Look carefully at what the vet is doing

Carrying box in which your pet feels safe while travelling

My pet's fact sheet

Try making a fact sheet about each of your birds. Copy the headings on this page or you can make up your own. Then write in the correct information about your bird.

Throat spots

Blue cere

Green chest

Black wing markings

Grey claws

Leave a space to stick in a photograph or draw a picture of each of your pets. Then label all of your pet's special features.

Name: **Charlie**

Birthday: **1st November**

Weight: **40g (1½ oz)**

Favourite fresh food: **Spinach**

Best friend: **George**

Vet's name: **Mark Evans**

Nurse's name: **Sarah Ponder**

Vet centre telephone number: **089582 2324**

Index